SELF CARE PLANNER & JOURNAL FOR BLACK WOMEN

SIMPLE SELF CARE ORGANIZER & REFLECTIVE JOURNAL TO GET YOURSELF TOGETHER

CHECK OUT OUR OTHER SELF CARE BOOKS

SELF CARE WORKBOOK FOR BLACK WOMEN

A 120+ page activity book covering mental, physical, spiritual and emotional self help practices. Complete with a 12-month planner and guided journal

EMOTIONAL SELF CARE FOR BLACK WOMEN

A self help activity book to address the thoughts, beliefs and triggers which affect your emotions and behavior

SPIRITUAL SELF CARE FOR BLACK WOMEN

A guided journal and 12-month planner with more in-depth self reflection and spirituality activities

Stress Less Press are a Black-owned independent publisher. If you enjoy this book, please consider supporting us by leaving a review on Amazon!

INTRODUCTION

LET'S TALK ABOUT YOUR SELF CARE

Well firstly, what do we mean by self care? Self care refers to the activities and practices you take part in with the purpose of enhancing your health and wellbeing. It's a pretty broad concept that encompasses everything from your nutrition to lifestyle to interpersonal relationships, with the main pillars being mental, physical, spiritual, social and emotional self care.

Ultimately, self care will mean different things for different people; it's about developing healthy habits that are meaningful to **you**, and sustainable for **you**.

Self care is about connecting with your wants, needs and passions, and prioritizing time for these things in your life. It's also about self awareness, and understanding the stressors that may be causing you to feel unwell, whether that be physically, mentally or emotionally.

We know that self care involves looking after yourself mentally, physically, spiritually, socially and emotionally. Now, that's a lot! The best way to make sure we don't fall off, is to actively plan ahead. That's why we've created this planner; so you can intentionally make time your self care activities and be accountable to yourself – just like you would any other life commitment. Each week you can take the time to plan what you are going to do each day, both in terms of self care activities, and working towards general goals and priorities. While helping you to build daily self care habits, the book also has space for self reflection each week with prompts provided.

Despite what we're taught, self care isn't selfish and you deserve to focus on it on a daily basis. So start planning Sis, turn the page and begin your self care journey.

SELF CARE ACTIVITIES

SOME IDEAS TO TRY OUT

MENTAL SELF CARE

- Take a 1-day break from social media
- Engage in a non-work hobby
- Read a book for 15 minutes every night for a full week

PHYSICAL SELF CARE

- Do a week's worth of healthy meal prep
- Use your sick leave
- Eat lunch away from your desk
- Attend a yoga class

SPIRITUAL SELF CARE

- Identify what nurtures your spirit
- Practice meditation
- Reward yourself
- Cleanse your space
- Create a vision board

EMOTIONAL SELF CARE

- Attend a therapy session
- Set boundaries with people
- Let your feelings out in a journal

SOCIAL SELF CARE

- Host an online quiz night
- Reconnect with an old friend
- Create a care package for your favorite person
- Go on a date
- Volunteer in your local area

For more self care ideas and activities, check out the other books in our series!

Take yourself off the back burner, Sis

STRESS LESS PRESS

W/C:

PLANNING AHEAD

	GOALS & PRIORITIES	SELF CARE ACTIVITIES
MON		
TUES		
WED		
THU		
FRI		
SAT		
SUN		

LOOKING BACK

✦ What did I do to take care of myself this week?

_____

_____

✦ What brought me joy this week?

_____

_____

✦ What did I find challenging this week, and how did I deal with it?

_____

_____

✦ What did I do to step out of my comfort zone this week?

_____

_____

✦ How have I practiced authenticity this week?

_____

_____

✦ What am I thankful for this week?

_____

_____

✦ Is there any baggage (emotional or otherwise) I can drop before starting a new week?

_____

_____

PLANNING AHEAD

	GOALS & PRIORITIES	SELF CARE ACTIVITIES
MON		
TUES		
WED		
THU		
FRI		
SAT		
SUN		

LOOKING BACK

✧ What did I do to take care of myself this week?

_____

_____

✧ What brought me joy this week?

_____

_____

✧ What did I find challenging this week, and how did I deal with it?

_____

_____

✧ What did I do to step out of my comfort zone this week?

_____

_____

✧ How have I practiced authenticity this week?

_____

_____

✧ What am I thankful for this week?

_____

_____

✧ Is there any baggage (emotional or otherwise) I can drop before starting a new week?

_____

_____

W/C:

PLANNING AHEAD

	GOALS & PRIORITIES	**SELF CARE ACTIVITIES**
MON		
TUES		
WED		
THU		
FRI		
SAT		
SUN		

LOOKING BACK

✦ What did I do to take care of myself this week?

_____

_____

✦ What brought me joy this week?

_____

_____

✦ What did I find challenging this week, and how did I deal with it?

_____

_____

✦ What did I do to step out of my comfort zone this week?

_____

_____

✦ How have I practiced authenticity this week?

_____

_____

✦ What am I thankful for this week?

_____

_____

✦ Is there any baggage (emotional or otherwise) I can drop before starting a new week?

_____

_____

W/C:

PLANNING AHEAD

	GOALS & PRIORITIES	SELF CARE ACTIVITIES
MON		
TUES		
WED		
THU		
FRI		
SAT		
SUN		

LOOKING BACK

✧ What did I do to take care of myself this week?

_____
_____

✧ What brought me joy this week?

_____
_____

✧ What did I find challenging this week, and how did I deal with it?

_____
_____

✧ What did I do to step out of my comfort zone this week?

_____
_____

✧ How have I practiced authenticity this week?

_____
_____

✧ What am I thankful for this week?

_____
_____

✧ Is there any baggage (emotional or otherwise) I can drop before starting a new week?

_____
_____

W/C:

PLANNING AHEAD

GOALS & PRIORITIES   ## SELF CARE ACTIVITIES

MON

TUES

WED

THU

FRI

SAT

SUN

LOOKING BACK

✦ What did I do to take care of myself this week?

_____

_____

✦ What brought me joy this week?

_____

_____

✦ What did I find challenging this week, and how did I deal with it?

_____

_____

✦ What did I do to step out of my comfort zone this week?

_____

_____

✦ How have I practiced authenticity this week?

_____

_____

✦ What am I thankful for this week?

_____

_____

✦ Is there any baggage (emotional or otherwise) I can drop before starting a new week?

_____

_____

PLANNING AHEAD

GOALS & PRIORITIES	SELF CARE ACTIVITIES
MON	
TUES	
WED	
THU	
FRI	
SAT	
SUN	

LOOKING BACK

✦ What did I do to take care of myself this week?

_____

_____

✦ What brought me joy this week?

_____

_____

✦ What did I find challenging this week, and how did I deal with it?

_____

_____

✦ What did I do to step out of my comfort zone this week?

_____

_____

✦ How have I practiced authenticity this week?

_____

_____

✦ What am I thankful for this week?

_____

_____

✦ Is there any baggage (emotional or otherwise) I can drop before starting a new week?

_____

_____

W/C:

PLANNING AHEAD

	GOALS & PRIORITIES	SELF CARE ACTIVITIES
MON		
TUES		
WED		
THU		
FRI		
SAT		
SUN		

LOOKING BACK

✧ What did I do to take care of myself this week?

_____

_____

✧ What brought me joy this week?

_____

_____

✧ What did I find challenging this week, and how did I deal with it?

_____

_____

✧ What did I do to step out of my comfort zone this week?

_____

_____

✧ How have I practiced authenticity this week?

_____

_____

✧ What am I thankful for this week?

_____

_____

✧ Is there any baggage (emotional or otherwise) I can drop before starting a new week?

_____

_____

W/C:

PLANNING AHEAD

	GOALS & PRIORITIES	SELF CARE ACTIVITIES
MON		
TUES		
WED		
THU		
FRI		
SAT		
SUN		

LOOKING BACK

✧ What did I do to take care of myself this week?

_____

_____

✧ What brought me joy this week?

_____

_____

✧ What did I find challenging this week, and how did I deal with it?

_____

_____

✧ What did I do to step out of my comfort zone this week?

_____

_____

✧ How have I practiced authenticity this week?

_____

_____

✧ What am I thankful for this week?

_____

_____

✧ Is there any baggage (emotional or otherwise) I can drop before starting a new week?

_____

_____

PLANNING AHEAD

	GOALS & PRIORITIES	SELF CARE ACTIVITIES
MON		
TUES		
WED		
THU		
FRI		
SAT		
SUN		

LOOKING BACK

✧ What did I do to take care of myself this week?

_____

_____

✧ What brought me joy this week?

_____

_____

✧ What did I find challenging this week, and how did I deal with it?

_____

_____

✧ What did I do to step out of my comfort zone this week?

_____

_____

✧ How have I practiced authenticity this week?

_____

_____

✧ What am I thankful for this week?

_____

_____

✧ Is there any baggage (emotional or otherwise) I can drop before starting a new week?

_____

_____

PLANNING AHEAD

	GOALS & PRIORITIES	**SELF CARE ACTIVITIES**
MON		
TUES		
WED		
THU		
FRI		
SAT		
SUN		

LOOKING BACK

✧ What did I do to take care of myself this week?

_____

_____

✧ What brought me joy this week?

_____

_____

✧ What did I find challenging this week, and how did I deal with it?

_____

_____

✧ What did I do to step out of my comfort zone this week?

_____

_____

✧ How have I practiced authenticity this week?

_____

_____

✧ What am I thankful for this week?

_____

_____

✧ Is there any baggage (emotional or otherwise) I can drop before starting a new week?

_____

_____

W/C:

PLANNING AHEAD

	GOALS & PRIORITIES	SELF CARE ACTIVITIES
MON		
TUES		
WED		
THU		
FRI		
SAT		
SUN		

LOOKING BACK

✧ What did I do to take care of myself this week?

_____

_____

✧ What brought me joy this week?

_____

_____

✧ What did I find challenging this week, and how did I deal with it?

_____

_____

✧ What did I do to step out of my comfort zone this week?

_____

_____

✧ How have I practiced authenticity this week?

_____

_____

✧ What am I thankful for this week?

_____

_____

✧ Is there any baggage (emotional or otherwise) I can drop before starting a new week?

_____

_____

PLANNING AHEAD

	GOALS & PRIORITIES	SELF CARE ACTIVITIES
MON		
TUES		
WED		
THU		
FRI		
SAT		
SUN		

LOOKING BACK

✧ What did I do to take care of myself this week?

_____

_____

✧ What brought me joy this week?

_____

_____

✧ What did I find challenging this week, and how did I deal with it?

_____

_____

✧ What did I do to step out of my comfort zone this week?

_____

_____

✧ How have I practiced authenticity this week?

_____

_____

✧ What am I thankful for this week?

_____

_____

✧ Is there any baggage (emotional or otherwise) I can drop before starting a new week?

_____

_____

PLANNING AHEAD

	GOALS & PRIORITIES	SELF CARE ACTIVITIES
MON		
TUES		
WED		
THU		
FRI		
SAT		
SUN		

LOOKING BACK

✧ What did I do to take care of myself this week?

_____

_____

✧ What brought me joy this week?

_____

_____

✧ What did I find challenging this week, and how did I deal with it?

_____

_____

✧ What did I do to step out of my comfort zone this week?

_____

_____

✧ How have I practiced authenticity this week?

_____

_____

✧ What am I thankful for this week?

_____

_____

✧ Is there any baggage (emotional or otherwise) I can drop before starting a new week?

_____

_____

W/C:

PLANNING AHEAD

	GOALS & PRIORITIES	SELF CARE ACTIVITIES
MON		
TUES		
WED		
THU		
FRI		
SAT		
SUN		

LOOKING BACK

✦ What did I do to take care of myself this week?

_____

_____

✦ What brought me joy this week?

_____

_____

✦ What did I find challenging this week, and how did I deal with it?

_____

_____

✦ What did I do to step out of my comfort zone this week?

_____

_____

✦ How have I practiced authenticity this week?

_____

_____

✦ What am I thankful for this week?

_____

_____

✦ Is there any baggage (emotional or otherwise) I can drop before starting a new week?

_____

_____

PLANNING AHEAD

	GOALS & PRIORITIES	SELF CARE ACTIVITIES
MON		
TUES		
WED		
THU		
FRI		
SAT		
SUN		

LOOKING BACK

✦ What did I do to take care of myself this week?

_____

_____

✦ What brought me joy this week?

_____

_____

✦ What did I find challenging this week, and how did I deal with it?

_____

_____

✦ What did I do to step out of my comfort zone this week?

_____

_____

✦ How have I practiced authenticity this week?

_____

_____

✦ What am I thankful for this week?

_____

_____

✦ Is there any baggage (emotional or otherwise) I can drop before starting a new week?

_____

_____

W/C:

PLANNING AHEAD

	GOALS & PRIORITIES	SELF CARE ACTIVITIES
MON		
TUES		
WED		
THU		
FRI		
SAT		
SUN		

LOOKING BACK

✧ What did I do to take care of myself this week?

_____

_____

✧ What brought me joy this week?

_____

_____

✧ What did I find challenging this week, and how did I deal with it?

_____

_____

✧ What did I do to step out of my comfort zone this week?

_____

_____

✧ How have I practiced authenticity this week?

_____

_____

✧ What am I thankful for this week?

_____

_____

✧ Is there any baggage (emotional or otherwise) I can drop before starting a new week?

_____

_____

W/C:

PLANNING AHEAD

	GOALS & PRIORITIES	SELF CARE ACTIVITIES
MON		
TUES		
WED		
THU		
FRI		
SAT		
SUN		

LOOKING BACK

✧ What did I do to take care of myself this week?

_____

_____

✧ What brought me joy this week?

_____

_____

✧ What did I find challenging this week, and how did I deal with it?

_____

_____

✧ What did I do to step out of my comfort zone this week?

_____

_____

✧ How have I practiced authenticity this week?

_____

_____

✧ What am I thankful for this week?

_____

_____

✧ Is there any baggage (emotional or otherwise) I can drop before starting a new week?

_____

_____

W/C:

PLANNING AHEAD

GOALS & PRIORITIES

SELF CARE ACTIVITIES

MON

TUES

WED

THU

FRI

SAT

SUN

LOOKING BACK

✧ What did I do to take care of myself this week?

_____

_____

✧ What brought me joy this week?

_____

_____

✧ What did I find challenging this week, and how did I deal with it?

_____

_____

✧ What did I do to step out of my comfort zone this week?

_____

_____

✧ How have I practiced authenticity this week?

_____

_____

✧ What am I thankful for this week?

_____

_____

✧ Is there any baggage (emotional or otherwise) I can drop before starting a new week?

_____

_____

PLANNING AHEAD

	GOALS & PRIORITIES	SELF CARE ACTIVITIES
MON		
TUES		
WED		
THU		
FRI		
SAT		
SUN		

LOOKING BACK

✦ What did I do to take care of myself this week?

_____

_____

✦ What brought me joy this week?

_____

_____

✦ What did I find challenging this week, and how did I deal with it?

_____

_____

✦ What did I do to step out of my comfort zone this week?

_____

_____

✦ How have I practiced authenticity this week?

_____

_____

✦ What am I thankful for this week?

_____

_____

✦ Is there any baggage (emotional or otherwise) I can drop before starting a new week?

_____

_____

PLANNING AHEAD

	GOALS & PRIORITIES	SELF CARE ACTIVITIES
MON		
TUES		
WED		
THU		
FRI		
SAT		
SUN		

LOOKING BACK

✧ What did I do to take care of myself this week?

_____

_____

✧ What brought me joy this week?

_____

_____

✧ What did I find challenging this week, and how did I deal with it?

_____

_____

✧ What did I do to step out of my comfort zone this week?

_____

_____

✧ How have I practiced authenticity this week?

_____

_____

✧ What am I thankful for this week?

_____

_____

✧ Is there any baggage (emotional or otherwise) I can drop before starting a new week?

_____

_____

PLANNING AHEAD

	GOALS & PRIORITIES	SELF CARE ACTIVITIES
MON		
TUES		
WED		
THU		
FRI		
SAT		
SUN		

LOOKING BACK

✧ What did I do to take care of myself this week?

_____

_____

✧ What brought me joy this week?

_____

_____

✧ What did I find challenging this week, and how did I deal with it?

_____

_____

✧ What did I do to step out of my comfort zone this week?

_____

_____

✧ How have I practiced authenticity this week?

_____

_____

✧ What am I thankful for this week?

_____

_____

✧ Is there any baggage (emotional or otherwise) I can drop before starting a new week?

_____

_____

W/C:

PLANNING AHEAD

	GOALS & PRIORITIES	SELF CARE ACTIVITIES
MON		
TUES		
WED		
THU		
FRI		
SAT		
SUN		

LOOKING BACK

✦ What did I do to take care of myself this week?

_____

_____

✦ What brought me joy this week?

_____

_____

✦ What did I find challenging this week, and how did I deal with it?

_____

_____

✦ What did I do to step out of my comfort zone this week?

_____

_____

✦ How have I practiced authenticity this week?

_____

_____

✦ What am I thankful for this week?

_____

_____

✦ Is there any baggage (emotional or otherwise) I can drop before starting a new week?

_____

_____

W/C:

PLANNING AHEAD

	GOALS & PRIORITIES	SELF CARE ACTIVITIES
MON		
TUES		
WED		
THU		
FRI		
SAT		
SUN		

LOOKING BACK

✦ What did I do to take care of myself this week?

_____

_____

✦ What brought me joy this week?

_____

_____

✦ What did I find challenging this week, and how did I deal with it?

_____

_____

✦ What did I do to step out of my comfort zone this week?

_____

_____

✦ How have I practiced authenticity this week?

_____

_____

✦ What am I thankful for this week?

_____

_____

✦ Is there any baggage (emotional or otherwise) I can drop before starting a new week?

_____

_____

W/C:

PLANNING AHEAD

	GOALS & PRIORITIES	SELF CARE ACTIVITIES
MON		
TUES		
WED		
THU		
FRI		
SAT		
SUN		

LOOKING BACK

✧ What did I do to take care of myself this week?

_____

_____

✧ What brought me joy this week?

_____

_____

✧ What did I find challenging this week, and how did I deal with it?

_____

_____

✧ What did I do to step out of my comfort zone this week?

_____

_____

✧ How have I practiced authenticity this week?

_____

_____

✧ What am I thankful for this week?

_____

_____

✧ Is there any baggage (emotional or otherwise) I can drop before starting a new week?

_____

_____

PLANNING AHEAD

	GOALS & PRIORITIES	SELF CARE ACTIVITIES
MON		
TUES		
WED		
THU		
FRI		
SAT		
SUN		

LOOKING BACK

✦ What did I do to take care of myself this week?

_____

_____

✦ What brought me joy this week?

_____

_____

✦ What did I find challenging this week, and how did I deal with it?

_____

_____

✦ What did I do to step out of my comfort zone this week?

_____

_____

✦ How have I practiced authenticity this week?

_____

_____

✦ What am I thankful for this week?

_____

_____

✦ Is there any baggage (emotional or otherwise) I can drop before starting a new week?

_____

_____

W/C:

PLANNING AHEAD

	GOALS & PRIORITIES	SELF CARE ACTIVITIES
MON		
TUES		
WED		
THU		
FRI		
SAT		
SUN		

LOOKING BACK

✦ What did I do to take care of myself this week?

_____

_____

✦ What brought me joy this week?

_____

_____

✦ What did I find challenging this week, and how did I deal with it?

_____

_____

✦ What did I do to step out of my comfort zone this week?

_____

_____

✦ How have I practiced authenticity this week?

_____

_____

✦ What am I thankful for this week?

_____

_____

✦ Is there any baggage (emotional or otherwise) I can drop before starting a new week?

_____

_____

W/C:

PLANNING AHEAD

	GOALS & PRIORITIES	SELF CARE ACTIVITIES
MON		
TUES		
WED		
THU		
FRI		
SAT		
SUN		

LOOKING BACK

✦ What did I do to take care of myself this week?

_____

_____

✦ What brought me joy this week?

_____

_____

✦ What did I find challenging this week, and how did I deal with it?

_____

_____

✦ What did I do to step out of my comfort zone this week?

_____

_____

✦ How have I practiced authenticity this week?

_____

_____

✦ What am I thankful for this week?

_____

_____

✦ Is there any baggage (emotional or otherwise) I can drop before starting a new week?

_____

_____

W/C:

PLANNING AHEAD

	GOALS & PRIORITIES	SELF CARE ACTIVITIES
MON		
TUES		
WED		
THU		
FRI		
SAT		
SUN		

LOOKING BACK

✧ What did I do to take care of myself this week?

_____

_____

✧ What brought me joy this week?

_____

_____

✧ What did I find challenging this week, and how did I deal with it?

_____

_____

✧ What did I do to step out of my comfort zone this week?

_____

_____

✧ How have I practiced authenticity this week?

_____

_____

✧ What am I thankful for this week?

_____

_____

✧ Is there any baggage (emotional or otherwise) I can drop before starting a new week?

_____

_____

W/C:

PLANNING AHEAD

	GOALS & PRIORITIES	SELF CARE ACTIVITIES
MON		
TUES		
WED		
THU		
FRI		
SAT		
SUN		

LOOKING BACK

✦ What did I do to take care of myself this week?

_____

_____

✦ What brought me joy this week?

_____

_____

✦ What did I find challenging this week, and how did I deal with it?

_____

_____

✦ What did I do to step out of my comfort zone this week?

_____

_____

✦ How have I practiced authenticity this week?

_____

_____

✦ What am I thankful for this week?

_____

_____

✦ Is there any baggage (emotional or otherwise) I can drop before starting a new week?

_____

_____

W/C:

PLANNING AHEAD

	GOALS & PRIORITIES	SELF CARE ACTIVITIES
MON		
TUES		
WED		
THU		
FRI		
SAT		
SUN		

LOOKING BACK

✧ What did I do to take care of myself this week?

_____

_____

✧ What brought me joy this week?

_____

_____

✧ What did I find challenging this week, and how did I deal with it?

_____

_____

✧ What did I do to step out of my comfort zone this week?

_____

_____

✧ How have I practiced authenticity this week?

_____

_____

✧ What am I thankful for this week?

_____

_____

✧ Is there any baggage (emotional or otherwise) I can drop before starting a new week?

_____

_____

W/C:

PLANNING AHEAD

GOALS & PRIORITIES	SELF CARE ACTIVITIES
MON	
TUES	
WED	
THU	
FRI	
SAT	
SUN	

LOOKING BACK

✦ What did I do to take care of myself this week?

_____

_____

✦ What brought me joy this week?

_____

_____

✦ What did I find challenging this week, and how did I deal with it?

_____

_____

✦ What did I do to step out of my comfort zone this week?

_____

_____

✦ How have I practiced authenticity this week?

_____

_____

✦ What am I thankful for this week?

_____

_____

✦ Is there any baggage (emotional or otherwise) I can drop before starting a new week?

_____

_____

W/C:

PLANNING AHEAD

	GOALS & PRIORITIES	SELF CARE ACTIVITIES
MON		
TUES		
WED		
THU		
FRI		
SAT		
SUN		

LOOKING BACK

✦ What did I do to take care of myself this week?

_____

_____

✦ What brought me joy this week?

_____

_____

✦ What did I find challenging this week, and how did I deal with it?

_____

_____

✦ What did I do to step out of my comfort zone this week?

_____

_____

✦ How have I practiced authenticity this week?

_____

_____

✦ What am I thankful for this week?

_____

_____

✦ Is there any baggage (emotional or otherwise) I can drop before starting a new week?

_____

_____

W/C:

PLANNING AHEAD

GOALS & PRIORITIES

SELF CARE ACTIVITIES

MON

TUES

WED

THU

FRI

SAT

SUN

LOOKING BACK

✦ What did I do to take care of myself this week?

_____

_____

✦ What brought me joy this week?

_____

_____

✦ What did I find challenging this week, and how did I deal with it?

_____

_____

✦ What did I do to step out of my comfort zone this week?

_____

_____

✦ How have I practiced authenticity this week?

_____

_____

✦ What am I thankful for this week?

_____

_____

✦ Is there any baggage (emotional or otherwise) I can drop before starting a new week?

_____

_____

W/C:

PLANNING AHEAD

	GOALS & PRIORITIES	SELF CARE ACTIVITIES
MON		
TUES		
WED		
THU		
FRI		
SAT		
SUN		

LOOKING BACK

✦ What did I do to take care of myself this week?

_____

_____

✦ What brought me joy this week?

_____

_____

✦ What did I find challenging this week, and how did I deal with it?

_____

_____

✦ What did I do to step out of my comfort zone this week?

_____

_____

✦ How have I practiced authenticity this week?

_____

_____

✦ What am I thankful for this week?

_____

_____

✦ Is there any baggage (emotional or otherwise) I can drop before starting a new week?

_____

_____

PLANNING AHEAD

GOALS & PRIORITIES

SELF CARE ACTIVITIES

MON

TUES

WED

THU

FRI

SAT

SUN

LOOKING BACK

✦ What did I do to take care of myself this week?

_____

_____

✦ What brought me joy this week?

_____

_____

✦ What did I find challenging this week, and how did I deal with it?

_____

_____

✦ What did I do to step out of my comfort zone this week?

_____

_____

✦ How have I practiced authenticity this week?

_____

_____

✦ What am I thankful for this week?

_____

_____

✦ Is there any baggage (emotional or otherwise) I can drop before starting a new week?

_____

_____

DATE:

NOTES

NOTES

NOTES

DATE:

NOTES

NOTES

NOTES

DATE:

NOTES

DATE:

NOTES

NOTES

DATE:

NOTES

NOTES

DATE:

NOTES

DATE:

NOTES

NOTES

NOTES

DATE:

NOTES

DATE:

NOTES

DATE:

NOTES

DATE:

NOTES

DATE:

NOTES

DATE:

NOTES

Made in the USA
Coppell, TX
08 April 2024

31057739R00057